all woman JAZZ

Series Editor: Anna Joyce
Production Editor: Chris Harvey
Editorial, production and recording: Artemis Music Limited
Design and Production: Space DPS Limited

Published 2001

International
MUSIC
Publications

© International Music Publications Limited
Griffin House 161 Hammersmith Road London W6 8BS England

Reproducing this music in any form is illegal and forbidden by
the Copyright, Designs and Patents Act 1988

Bewitched

Words by Lorenz Hart
Music by Richard Rodgers

© 1941 Chappell & Co Inc, USA
Warner/Chappell Music Ltd, London W6 8BS

Dream A Little Dream Of Me

Words by Gus Kahn
Music by Fabian Andre and Wilbur Schwandt

Track 2
Backing

© 1931 Words And Music Inc, USA

Francis Day & Hunter Ltd, London WC2H 0QY and EMI Music Publishing Ltd, London WC2H 0QY

Dream a lit-tle dream of me.

Dream a lit-tle dream of me.

A Foggy Day

Music and Lyrics by George Gershwin and Ira Gershwin

© 1937 (Renewed 1964) George Gershwin Music and Ira Gershwin Music, USA
Warner/Chappell Music Ltd, London W6 8BS

Track 4
Backing

The Girl From Ipanema

Original Words by Vinicius de Moraes
English Words by Norman Gimbel
Music by Antonio Carlos Jobim

Moderate Bossa Nova

Lyrics:

Tall and tan and young and { love-ly, the girl / hand-some the boy } from I-pa-ne-ma goes walk-ing, and when { she pass-es, each one she / he pass-es, each girl he } pass-es goes "aah!" When { she walks it's / he walks he's } like—

© 1963 Antonio Carlos Jobim and Vinicius de Moraes, Brazil
Universal/MCA Music Ltd, London W6 8JA

I'm In The Mood For Love

Words by Dorothy Fields
Music by Jimmy McHugh

© 1935 EMI Catalogue Partnership, EMI Robbins Catalog Inc and EMI United Partnership Ltd, USA
Worldwide print rights controlled by Warner Bros Publications Inc/IMP Ltd

In The Mood

Words by Andy Razaf
Music by Joe Garland

In the groove

Mis - ter What - cha - call - um, what - cha
Mis - ter What - cha - call - um, all you

do - in' to - night?___ Hope you're in the mood be - cause I'm feel - in' just right.___
need - ed was fun.___ You can see the won - ders that this ev - 'nin' has done.___

© 1939 Shapiro Bernstein & Co Inc, USA
Peter Maurice Music Co Ltd, London WC2H 0QY

Track 7
Backing

It Don't Mean A Thing
(If It Ain't Got That Swing)

Words by Irving Mills
Music by Duke Ellington

What good is me-lo-dy,— what good is mu-sic,—

© 1932 Gotham Music Service Inc and EMI Mills Music Inc, USA
Worldwide print rights controlled by Warner Bros Publications Inc/IMP Ltd

Misty

Backing

Words by Johnny Burke
Music by Erroll Garner

Slowly, with expression

© 1954 Octave Music Corp, Reganesque Music, Marke Music Pub Co Inc, Limerick Music Corp, Timoco Music and Spirit Two Music, USA
Warner/Chappell Music Ltd, London W6 8BS, Palan Music Publishing Ltd, London NW1 0AG and BMG Music Publishing Ltd, London SW6

3JW

Nice Work If You Can Get It

Music and Lyrics by George Gershwin and Ira Gershwin

Track 9
Backing

$\downarrow$ = 118

Lyrics:

Hold-ing hands at mid-night,— 'neath the star-ry sky,—

nice work if you can get it,——— and you can get it if— you try.—

Stroll-in' with the one boy,— sigh-ing sigh af-ter sigh,—

© 1937 (Renewed 1964) George Gershwin Music and Ira Gershwin Music, USA

Warner/Chappell Music Ltd, London W6 8BS

On Green Dolphin Street

Words by Ned Washington
Music by Bronislaw Kaper

© 1947 EMI Catalog Partnership, EMI United Partnership Ltd, USA
Worldwide print rights controlled by Warner Bros Publications Inc/IMP Ltd

'Round Midnight

Words and Music by Cootie Williams and Thelonious Monk

© 1944 Advanced Music Corp, USA
Warner/Chappell Music Ltd, London W6 8BS

Backing

Where Or When

Words by Lorenz Hart
Music by Richard Rodgers

Lyrics:

When you're a-wake the things you think come from the dreams you dream. Thought has wings, and lots of things are sel-dom what they seem. Some - times you think you've lived be - fore

© 1937 Chappell & Co Inc, USA
Warner/Chappell Music Ltd, London W6 8BS

Also Available

Heart and Soul:
New Songs from Ally McBeal
featuring Vonda Shepard
Piano/Vocal/Guitar
(7269A)   ISBN: 1859098649

More great songs from the Emmy Award-winning comedy! Titles are: Read Your Mind - 100 Tears Away - Someday We'll Be Together - To Sir, with Love (duet with Al Green) - Sweet Inspiration - Crying - Vincent (Starry Starry Night) - What Becomes of the Brokenhearted - Confetti - Baby Don't You Break My Heart Slow (duet with Emily Saliers of the Indigo Girls) - This Is Crazy Now - This Old Heart of Mine (Is Weak for You) - I Know Him by Heart - Searchin' My Soul.

Television Selections
featuring Vonda Shepard
Piano/Vocal/Guitar
(6704A)   ISBN: 1859096816

A collection of songs from the successful soundtrack album of the Emmy award-winning comedy series featuring the vocals of Vonda Shepard. Titles are: Searchin' My Soul - Ask the Lonely - Walk Away Renee - Hooked on a Feeling - You Belong to Me - The Wildest Times of the World - Someone You Use - The End of the World - Tell Him - Neighborhood - Will You Marry Me? - It's in His Kiss (The Shoop Shoop Song) - I Only Want to Be with You - Maryland.

Available now from all good music shops

AMB

Saw these fantastic books today! Must buy them immediately!

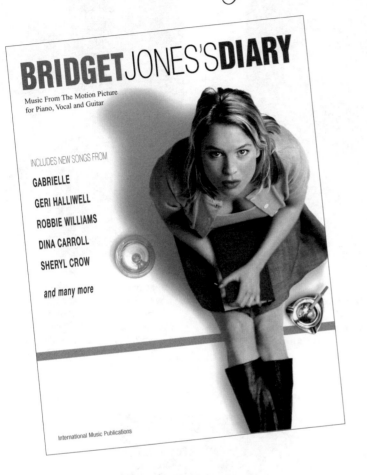

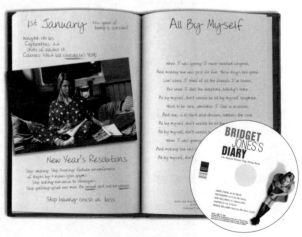

19 SONGS FROM THE MOTION PICTURE ARRANGED FOR PIANO, VOCAL AND GUITAR
9296A   ISBN 1-84328-017-5

GABRIELLE Out Of Reach
ARETHA FRANKLIN Respect
GERI HALLIWELL It's Raining Men
ROBBIE WILLIAMS Have You Met Miss Jones?
CHAKA KHAN I'm Every Woman
PRETENDERS Don't Get Me Wrong
SHERYL CROW Kiss That Girl
SHELBY LYNNE Killin' Kind
DINA CARROLL Someone Like You
ROBBIE WILLIAMS Not Of This Earth
ANDY WILLIAMS Can't Take My Eyes Off You
ROSEY Love
DIANA ROSS & MARVIN GAYE
Stop, Look, Listen (To Your Heart)
SHELBY LYNNE Dreamsome
PATRICK DOYLE It's Only A Diary
ALISHA'S ATTIC Pretender Got My Heart
JAMIE O'NEAL All By Myself
ARTFUL DODGER & ROBBIE CRAIG FEAT. CRAIG DAVID
Woman Trouble
AARON SOUL Ring, Ring, Ring

THE MOTION PICTURE SING-ALONG BOOK
5 SONGS WITH SING-ALONG CD
9537A   ISBN 1-84328-114-7

JAMIE O'NEAL All By Myself
PRETENDERS Don't Get Me Wrong
GERI HALLIWELL It's Raining Men
GABRIELLE Out Of Reach
ROBBIE WILLIAMS Have You Met Miss Jones?

AVAILABLE NOW FROM ALL GOOD MUSIC SHOPS

BJ1

YOU'RE THE VOICE

8861A PVC/CD

Casta Diva from Norma - Vissi D'arte from Tosca Un Bel Di Vedremo from Madam Butterfly - Addio, Del Passato from La Traviata - J'ai Perdu Mon Eurydice from Orphee Et Eurydice - Les Tringles Des Sistres Tintaient from Carmen - Porgi Amor from Le Nozze Di Figaro - Ave Maria from Otello

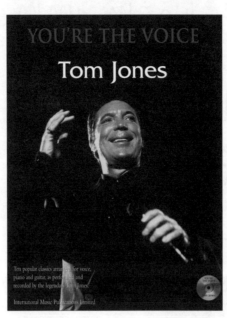

8860A PVG/CD

Delilah - Green Green Grass Of Home - Help Yourself - I'll Never Fall In Love Again - It's Not Unusual - Mama Told Me Not To Come - Sexbomb Thunderball - What's New Pussycat - You Can Leave Your Hat On

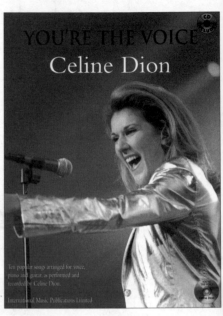

9297A PVG/CD

Beauty And The Beast - Because You Loved Me - Falling Into You - The First Time Ever I Saw Your Face - It's All Coming Back To Me Now - Misled - My Heart Will Go On - The Power Of Love - Think Twice - When I Fall In Love

9349A PVC/CD

Chain Of Fools - A Deeper Love Do Right Woman, Do Right Man - I Knew You Were Waiting (For Me) - I Never Loved A Man (The Way I Loved You) I Say A Little Prayer - Respect - Think Who's Zooming Who - (You Make Me Feel Like) A Natural Woman

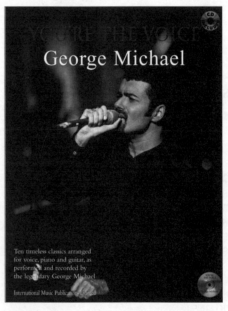

9007A PVC/CD

Careless Whisper - A Different Corner Faith - Father Figure - Freedom '90 I'm Your Man - I Knew You Were Waiting (For Me) - Jesus To A Child Older - Outside

The outstanding new vocal series from IMP

CD contains full backings for each song,
professionally arranged to recreate the sounds of the original recording